Color with Jesus

Devotional Coloring Book for Women

“NOW, BROTHERS AND SISTERS, I WANT TO REMIND
YOU OF THE GOSPEL I PREACHED TO YOU, WHICH YOU RECEIVED AND
ON WHICH YOU HAVE TAKEN YOUR STAND. 2 BY THIS GOSPEL YOU ARE
SAVED, IF YOU HOLD FIRMLY TO THE WORD I PREACHED TO YOU.
OTHERWISE, YOU HAVE BELIEVED IN VAIN. 3 FOR WHAT I RECEIVED I
PASSED ON TO YOU AS OF FIRST IMPORTANCE: THAT CHRIST DIED FOR
OUR SINS ACCORDING TO THE SCRIPTURES, 4 THAT HE WAS BURIED,
THAT HE WAS RAISED ON THE THIRD DAY ACCORDING TO THE
SCRIPTURES, 5 AND THAT HE APPEARED TO CEPHAS, AND THEN TO THE
TWELVE. 6 AFTER THAT, HE APPEARED TO MORE THAN FIVE HUNDRED
OF THE BROTHERS AND SISTERS AT THE SAME TIME, MOST OF WHOM
ARE STILL LIVING, THOUGH SOME HAVE FALLEN ASLEEP. 7 THEN HE
APPEARED TO JAMES, THEN TO ALL THE APOSTLES, 8 AND LAST OF ALL
HE APPEARED TO ME ALSO, AS TO ONE ABNORMALLY BORN.”

I CORINTHIANS 15: 1-8

THIS BOOK BELONGS TO

INTRODUCTION

The Lord wants a relationship with you. He wants you to pursue Him. Color with Jesus is much more than just a coloring book. It's designed to encourage you to spend time with Jesus. Read His scripture and meditate on His word. Whether you spend time alone or with others. Use Color with Jesus to deepen your relationship with the Lord, while you express your creative side!

Make sure to visit our website at www.colorwithjesus.com and sign up to receive updates on new book launches and some occasional inspiration. also make sure to follow us, you can find us on all social media @colorwithjesus.

HOW TO USE THIS BOOK

- I WOULD ENCOURAGE YOU TO HAVE YOUR BIBLE WITH YOU WHEN READING ANY VERSE. THIS WAY YOU CAN GO BACK AND READ THAT VERSE WITHIN CONTEXT OF WHAT WAS WRITTEN.

- THIS BOOK HAS A TOTAL OF 8 DEVOTIONAL TOPICS, WITH 5 BIBLE VERSES WITHIN THAT TOPIC. A TOTAL OF 40 BIBLE VERSES

- THERE IS A "WORDS FROM THE SPIRIT" WITH EACH PAGE, SO YOU CAN WRITE DOWN ANY THOUGHTS YOU FEEL THE LORD IS SPEAKING TO YOU

- COLOR WITH WHATEVER YOU'D LIKE. COLORED PENCILS OR GEL PENS WILL PROBABLY BE BEST. MARKER MAY BLEED THOUGH THE PAGE. THERE IS A "COLOR TEST PAGE" AT THE BACK, TO TEST FOR BLEED.

- WE WOULD LOVE TO SEE YOUR WORK. SO MAKE SURE TO POST IT ON SOCIAL MEDIA AND TAG US @COLORWITHJESUS

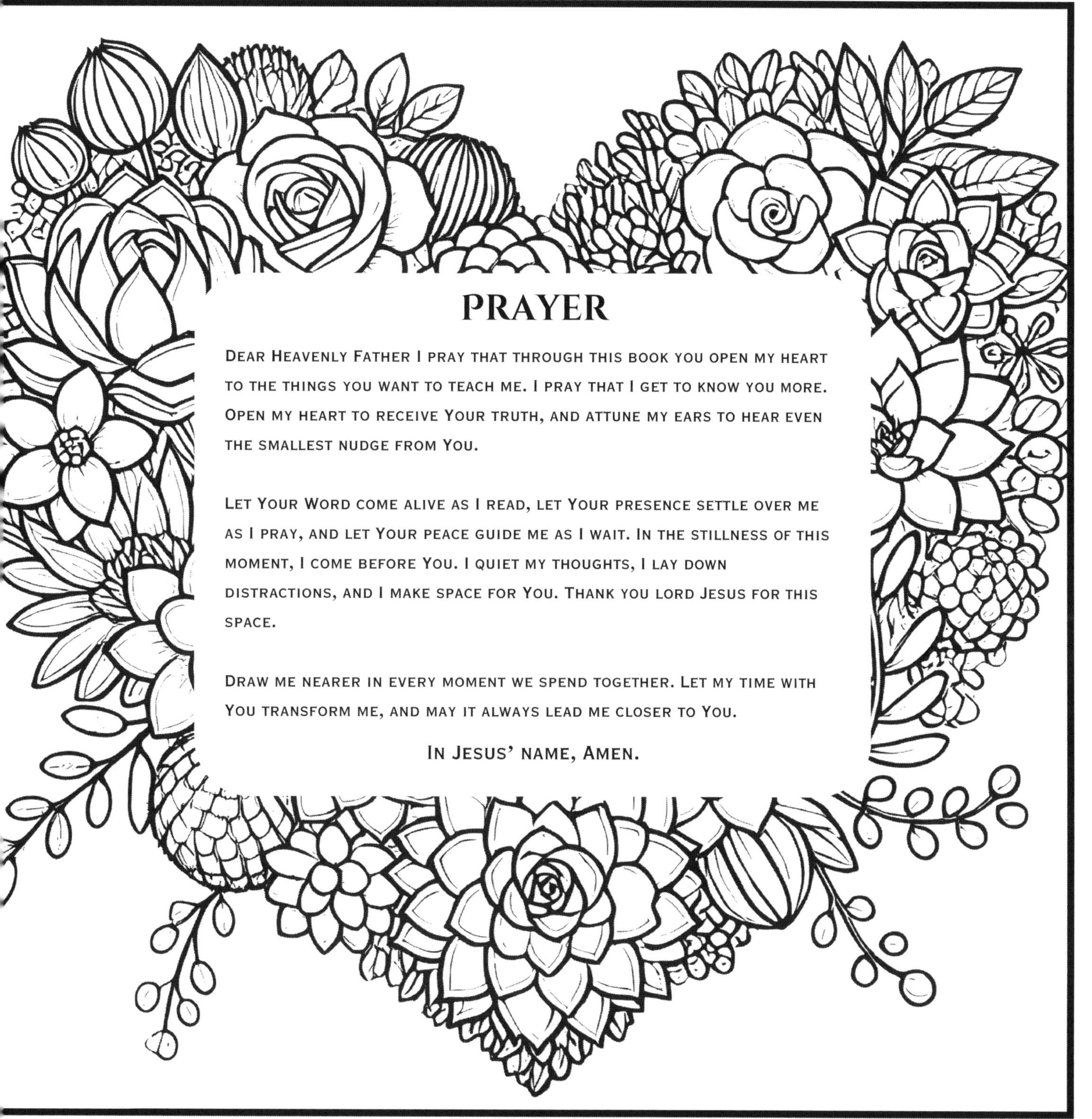

PRAYER

Dear Heavenly Father I pray that through this book you open my heart to the things you want to teach me. I pray that I get to know you more. Open my heart to receive Your truth, and attune my ears to hear even the smallest nudge from You.

Let Your Word come alive as I read, let Your presence settle over me as I pray, and let Your peace guide me as I wait. In the stillness of this moment, I come before You. I quiet my thoughts, I lay down distractions, and I make space for You. Thank you lord Jesus for this space.

Draw me nearer in every moment we spend together. Let my time with You transform me, and may it always lead me closer to You.

In Jesus' name, Amen.

Words from the Spirit

Hope & Encouragement

"Praise be to the God and Father of our Lord Jesus Christ! In his great mercy he has given us new birth into a living hope through the resurrection of Jesus Christ from the dead"

1 Peter 1:3

As believers, our hope is not a passive wish or fleeting desire. It is a living hope that is anchored in the resurrection of Jesus Christ. This hope is not based on circumstances, but on the reality of Christ's victory over death. Our hope is alive because Jesus is alive, and He promises that, no matter what we face, He is with us, offering us the strength to endure and the hope to carry on.

Father, thank you for the living hope we have through your resurrection. I place my hope in you, knowing that you have overcome death and that you will always be with me. When life feels difficult, remind me that my hope is secure in you, and you are my strength.
In Jesus' name, Amen.

Words from the Spirit

"For I know the plans I have for you, declares the Lord, plans to
prosper you and not to harm you, plans to give you hope and a future."
Jeremiah 29:11

WORDS FROM THE SPIRIT

"So do not fear, for I am with you; do not be dismayed, for I am your God. I will strengthen you and help you; I will uphold you with my righteous right hand."
Isaiah 41:10

Words from the Spirit

"May the God of hope fill you with
all joy and peace as you trust in
him, so that you may overflow
with hope by the power of the
Holy Spirit."
Romans 15:13

WORDS FROM THE SPIRIT

"I HAVE TOLD YOU THESE THINGS, SO THAT IN ME YOU MAY HAVE PEACE. IN THIS WORLD YOU WILL HAVE TROUBLE. BUT TAKE HEART! I HAVE OVERCOME THE WORLD."

JOHN 16:33

Words from the Spirit

Love & Relationships

"Do everything in love."

1 Corinthians 16:14

Love weaves throughout our lives, in every relationship. And in the way we love can truly impact those all around us. Love in its purest form goes beyond emotion, it is an action, a choice, and a reflection of God's love for us. Love is not just something we feel, but something we can actively choose to demonstrate, regardless of our circumstances. It can be easy to love when things are going well, but the true measure of love is often revealed in moments of conflict, disappointment, and challenges. When we love others in the same way that God loves us, we are choosing to serve and extend grace. The love that God offers us is limitless — it never runs dry, never grows weary. It is a love that stays, even when the road is difficult.

Father, thank you for loving me first, and unconditionally. I am grateful that my worth and value come from You alone. Help me to love others with the same depth and authenticity that You have shown me. May Your love fill me so that I can pour it out onto those around me regardless of my circumstances. In Jesus' name, Amen.

Words from the Spirit

"Dear friends, let us love one another, for love comes from God. Everyone who loves has been born of God and knows God. Whoever does not love does not know God, because God is love."

1 John 4:7-8

WORDS FROM THE SPIRIT

"Above all, love each other
deeply, because love covers
over a multitude of sins"
1 Peter 4:8

WORDS FROM THE SPIRIT

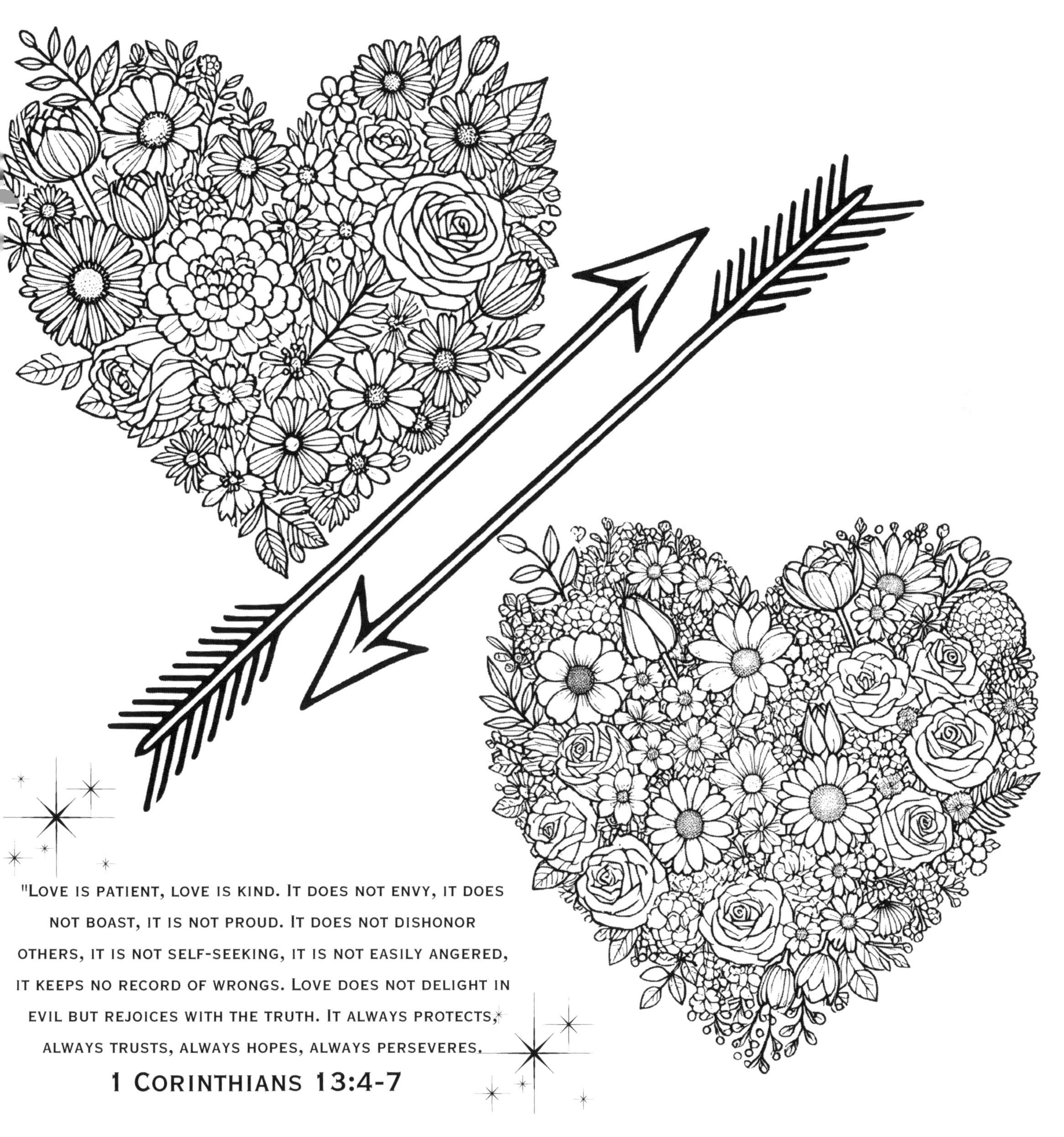
"Love is patient, love is kind. It does not envy, it does
not boast, it is not proud. It does not dishonor
others, it is not self-seeking, it is not easily angered,
it keeps no record of wrongs. Love does not delight in
evil but rejoices with the truth. It always protects,
always trusts, always hopes, always perseveres.
1 Corinthians 13:4-7

WORDS FROM THE SPIRIT

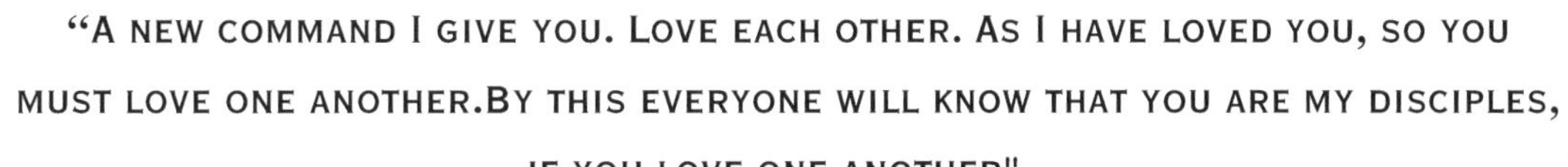

"A new command I give you. Love each other. As I have loved you, so you must love one another.By this everyone will know that you are my disciples, if you love one another"

John 13:34

WORDS FROM THE SPIRIT

Strength & Courage

"Have I not commanded you? Be strong and courageous. Do not be afraid; do not be discouraged, for the Lord your God will be with you wherever you go."

Joshua 1:9

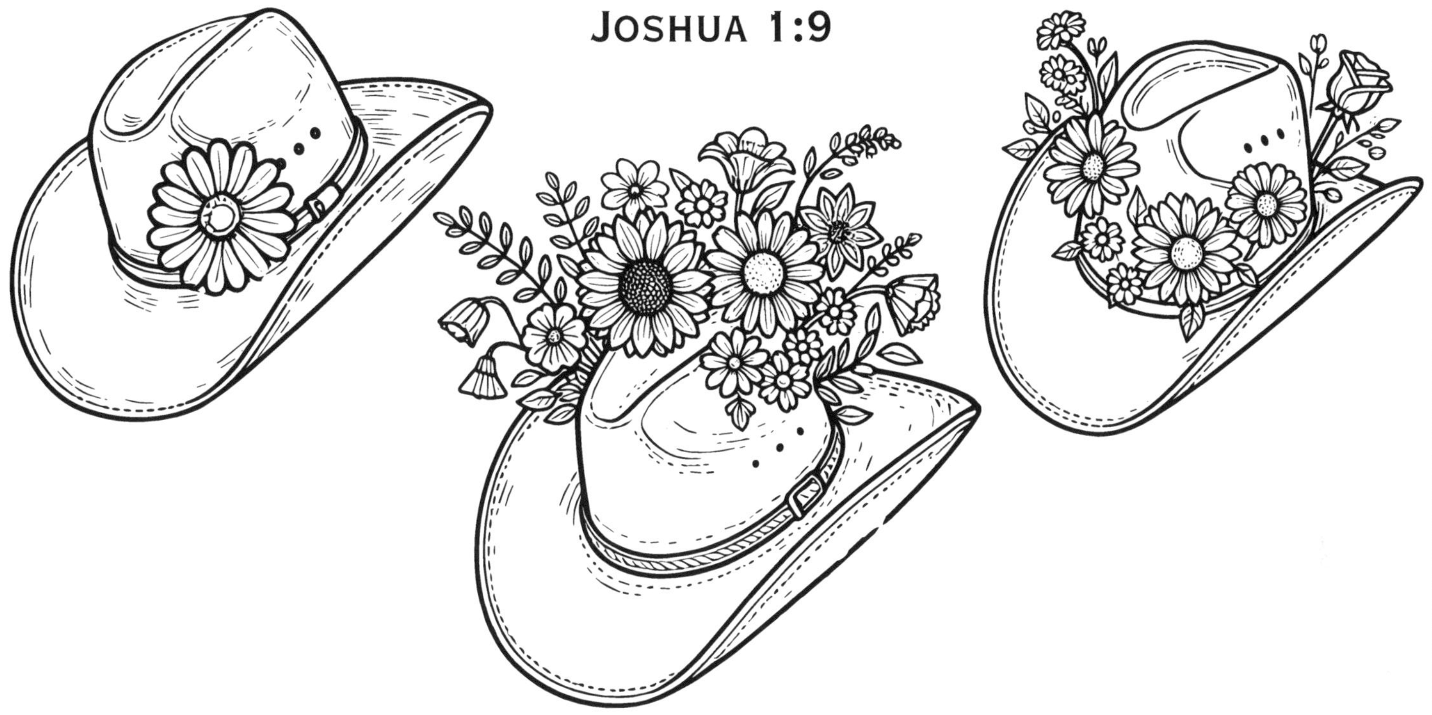

Stepping into the unknown often requires great courage. Throughout each new season in life, wether it be a new job, making a big decision, or maybe you're going through a difficult transition, fear can threaten to hold us back. But God calls us to be strong and courageous, trusting that He is with us every step of the way. When we face uncertainty, we can take comfort in knowing that God is not distant; He is present, guiding and strengthening us. Courage isn't the absence of fear but the willingness to move forward in faith despite it.

God, I ask for the courage to step forward into the unknown. Help me to trust that You are with me in every new situation, and that You will guide me. When fear arises, give me the strength to face it with faith. I choose to walk in courage, knowing that Your presence is my assurance.
In Jesus' name, Amen.

WORDS FROM THE SPIRIT

"It is because of him that you are in
Christ Jesus, who has become for us
wisdom from God—that is, our
righteousness, holiness and
redemption."
1 Corinthians 1:30

Words from the Spirit

"BUT THOSE WHO HOPE IN THE LORD WILL RENEW THEIR STRENGTH. THEY WILL SOAR ON WINGS LIKE EAGLES; THEY WILL RUN AND NOT GROW WEARY, THEY WILL WALK AND NOT BE FAINT."
ISAIAH 40:31

WORDS FROM THE SPIRIT

"For the Spirit God gave us does
not make us timid, but gives us
power, love and self-discipline."
2 Timothy 1:7

Words from the Spirit

"Be strong and courageous. Do not be afraid or
terrified because of them, for the Lord your God goes
with you; he will never leave you nor forsake you."
Deuteronomy 31:6

WORDS FROM THE SPIRIT

SERVING & PURPOSE

"FOR WE ARE GOD'S HANDIWORK, CREATED IN CHRIST JESUS TO DO GOOD WORKS, WHICH GOD PREPARED IN ADVANCE FOR US TO DO."

EPHESIANS 2:10

WE ARE OFTEN CALLED TO WEAR MANY HATS-DAUGHTER, WIFE, MOTHER, SISTER, FRIEND, BOSS, EMPLOYEE AND SO MUCH MORE. BUT IN ALL OF THESE ROLES, WE MUST REMEMBER THAT WE WERE CREATED BY GOD FOR A SPECIFIC PURPOSE. YOU ARE NOT HERE BY ACCIDENT; YOU ARE GOD'S MASTERPIECE. THE GOOD WORKS HE HAS PREPARED FOR YOU ARE UNIQUELY YOURS TO FULFILL. SERVING OTHERS IS NOT JUST ABOUT WHAT YOU DO; IT'S ABOUT EMBRACING THE PURPOSE GOD HAS DESIGNED FOR YOU. YOUR LIFE HAS MEANING, AND HE IS GUIDING YOU TO LIVE THAT OUT.

LORD, THANK YOU FOR CREATING ME WITH A PURPOSE. I KNOW THAT I AM YOUR HANDIWORK, AND YOU HAVE A PLAN FOR MY LIFE. HELP ME TO WALK IN THE GOOD WORKS YOU HAVE PREPARED FOR ME. GIVE ME THE STRENGTH AND COURAGE TO SERVE OTHERS WITH LOVE AND TO LIVE OUT MY PURPOSE FOR YOUR GLORY.
IN JESUS' NAME, AMEN.

WORDS FROM THE SPIRIT

"He has shown you, O
mortal, what is good. And
what does the Lord require
of you? To act justly and to
love mercy and to walk
humbly with your God."
Micah 6:8

WORDS FROM THE SPIRIT

"In the same way, let your light shine before others, that they may see your good deeds and glorify your Father in heaven."
Matthew 5:16

Words from the Spirit

"Therefore, my dear brothers and
sisters, stand firm. Let nothing
move you. Always give yourselves
fully to the work of the Lord,
because you know that your labor
in the Lord is not in vain."
1 Corinthians 15:58

Words from the Spirit

"Whatever you do, work at it with
all your heart, as working for the
Lord, not for human masters."
Colossians 3:23

WORDS FROM THE SPIRIT

Beauty & Worth

"Your beauty should not come from outward adornment, such as elaborate hairstyles and the wearing of gold jewelry or fine clothes. Rather, it should be that of your inner self, the unfading beauty of a gentle and quiet spirit, which is of great worth in God's sight."

1 Peter 3 3:4

We often find ourselves judging our worth based on external standards. The way we look, the clothes we wear, or the approval we receive from others. In a world that frequently ties beauty to physical appearance, it's easy to lose sight of the fact that our true beauty comes from within and is rooted in how God sees us!

Heavenly Father, thank you for creating me in your image. I praise you for the beauty you have woven into my life, both inside and out. Help me to see myself the way you see me, and remind me daily that my worth is found in your love, not in the world's standards. Strengthen me to live out my identity in you, and may my heart radiate the beauty of a gentle spirit that praises you.
In Jesus' name, Amen.

Words from the Spirit

“Charm is deceptive, and beauty is fleeting;
but a woman who fears the Lord is to be
praised.”
Proverbs 31:30

WORDS FROM THE SPIRIT

"For you created my inmost being; you knit me together in my mother's womb. I praise you because I am fearfully and wonderfully made; your works are wonderful, I know that full well."

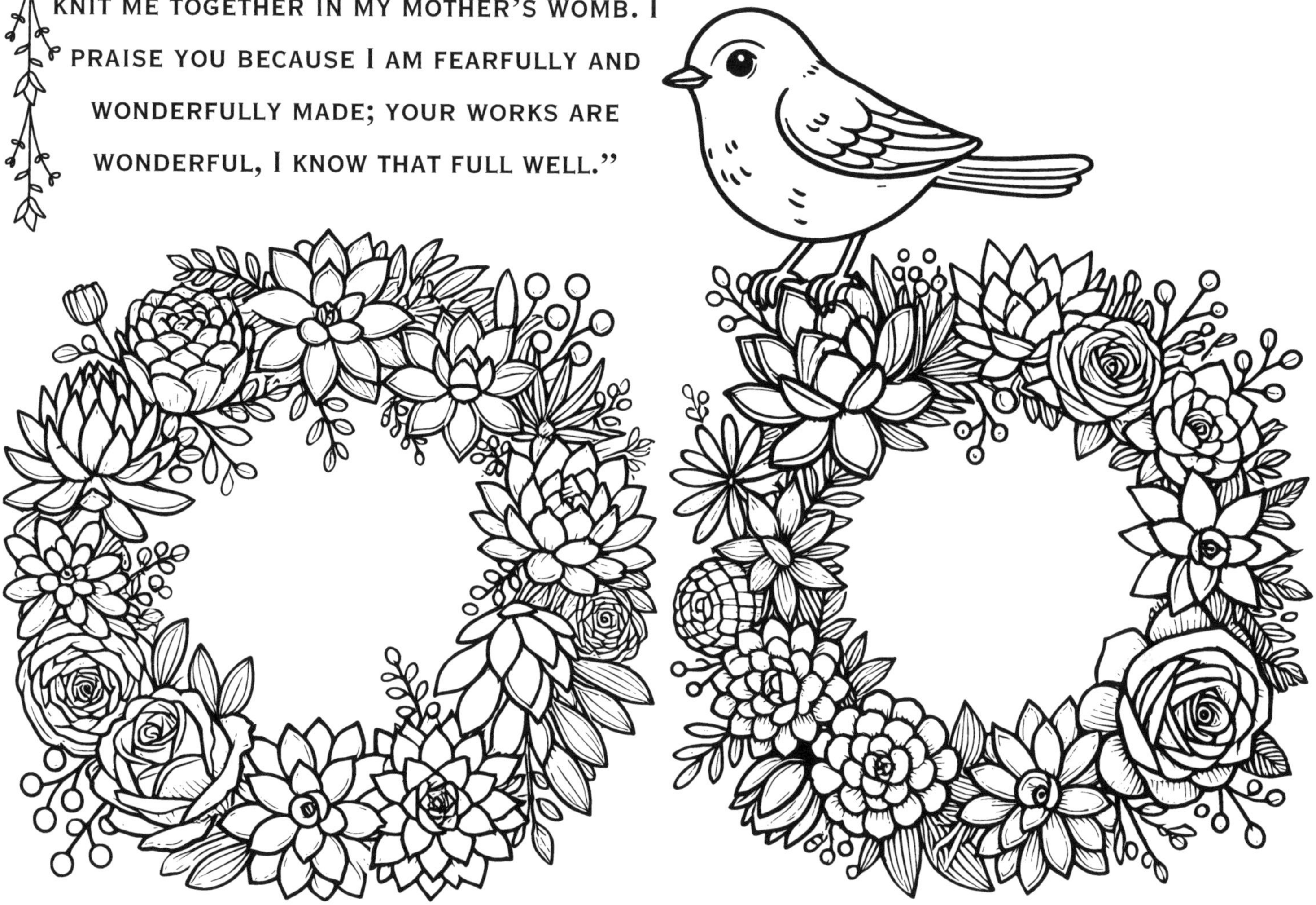

Psalms 139

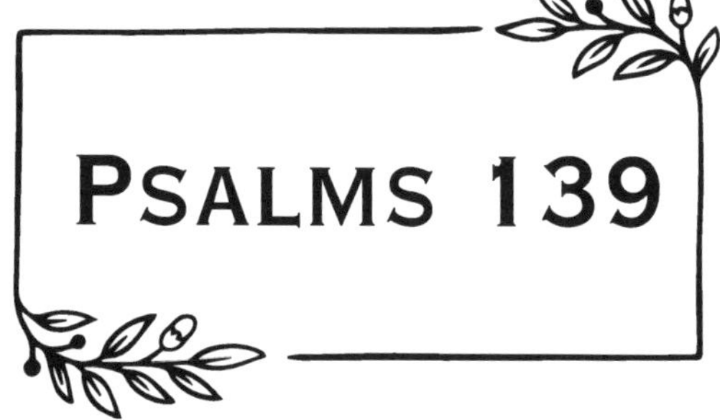

Words from the Spirit

"You are altogether
beautiful, my darling;
there is no flaw in you."
Song of Solomon 4:7

WORDS FROM THE SPIRIT

"The Lord does not
look at the things
people look at. People
look at the outward
appearance, but the
Lord looks at the
heart."
1 Samuel 16:7

WORDS FROM THE SPIRIT

Wisdom & Guidance

"Whether you turn to the right or to the left, your ears will hear a voice behind you, saying, 'This is the way; walk in it.'"

Isaiah 30:21

Life can often feel like a series of crossroads. And at times, we may find ourselves unsure of the direction to take. In these moments, God offers His wisdom and guidance in a personal and loving way. His voice is like a gentle whisper behind us, always directing us in the right direction. It may not always be loud, but the Holy Spirit is faithful to speak to our hearts, nudging us toward the way that leads to life. The key is to remain obedient and to be silent, to listen for his promptings, even in the midst of busy or uncertain times. When we listen for His voice, we will hear Him guiding us, even in our most challenging moments.

Lord, I come before You today asking for wisdom. Help me to seek Your guidance in all things. I trust that You will give me the wisdom I need to make decisions that honor You. Open my eyes and ears to Your truth and help me to discern Your will in every area of my life.
In Jesus' name, Amen

Words from the Spirit

"Your word is a lamp for my
feet, a light on my path."
Psalm 119:105

Words from the Spirit

"TRUST IN THE LORD WITH
ALL YOUR HEART AND LEAN
NOT ON YOUR OWN
UNDERSTANDING; IN ALL
YOUR WAYS SUBMIT TO HIM,
AND HE WILL MAKE YOUR
PATHS STRAIGHT."
PROVERBS 3:5-69

Words from the Spirit

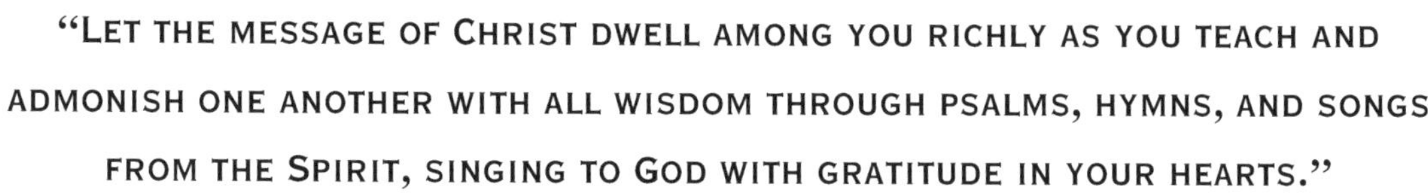

"Let the message of Christ dwell among you richly as you teach and admonish one another with all wisdom through psalms, hymns, and songs from the Spirit, singing to God with gratitude in your hearts."

Colossians 3:16

WORDS FROM THE SPIRIT

"If any of you lacks wisdom, you should ask God, who gives generously to all without finding fault, and it will be given to you."
James 1:5

WORDS FROM THE SPIRIT

MOTHERHOOD & FAMILY

"SHE IS CLOTHED WITH STRENGTH AND DIGNITY; SHE CAN LAUGH AT THE DAYS TO COME."

PROVERBS 31:25

AS MOTHERS, SISTERS, FRIENDS, WE ARE CALLED TO NURTURE AND CARE FOR OUR FAMILIES, AND IT TAKES GREAT STRENGTH TO DO SO. WHETHER IT'S OFFERING A LISTENING EAR, GIVING GUIDANCE, OR SIMPLY BEING THERE FOR YOUR FAMILY, YOUR ROLE IS VITAL. GOD EQUIPS YOU WITH THE STRENGTH TO RISE TO THE CHALLENGES OF EACH DAY. TRUST THAT HE WILL CONTINUE TO PROVIDE THE EMOTIONAL, SPIRITUAL, AND PHYSICAL STRENGTH YOU NEED TO NURTURE YOUR FAMILY.

LORD, THANK YOU FOR THE STRENGTH YOU PROVIDE IN MY ROLE AS A MOTHER, A SISTER, A FRIEND. HELP ME TO CARRY OUT MY RESPONSIBILITIES WITH DIGNITY AND GRACE. WHEN I FEEL WEARY, REMIND ME THAT YOU ARE MY SOURCE OF STRENGTH. GIVE ME THE COURAGE TO FACE EACH DAY WITH JOY AND CONFIDENCE, KNOWING THAT YOU ARE WITH ME EVERY STEP OF THE WAY.
IN JESUS' NAME, AMEN.

Words from the Spirit

"SHE SPEAKS WITH WISDOM, AND
FAITHFUL INSTRUCTION IS ON HER
TONGUE."
PROVERBS 31:26

Words from the Spirit

"These commandments that I give you today are to be on your hearts. Impress them on your children. Talk about them when you sit at home and when you walk along the road, when you lie down and when you get up."
Deuteronomy 6:6-7

Words from the Spirit

"Start children off on the way they should go, and even when they are old they will not turn from it."
Proverbs 22:6

WORDS FROM THE SPIRIT

"The wise woman builds her house, but
with her own hands the foolish one
tears hers down."
Proverbs 14:1

WORDS FROM THE SPIRIT

Faith & Trust

"Trust in the Lord with all your heart and lean not on your own understanding; in all your ways submit to Him, and He will make your paths straight."

Proverbs 3 5:6

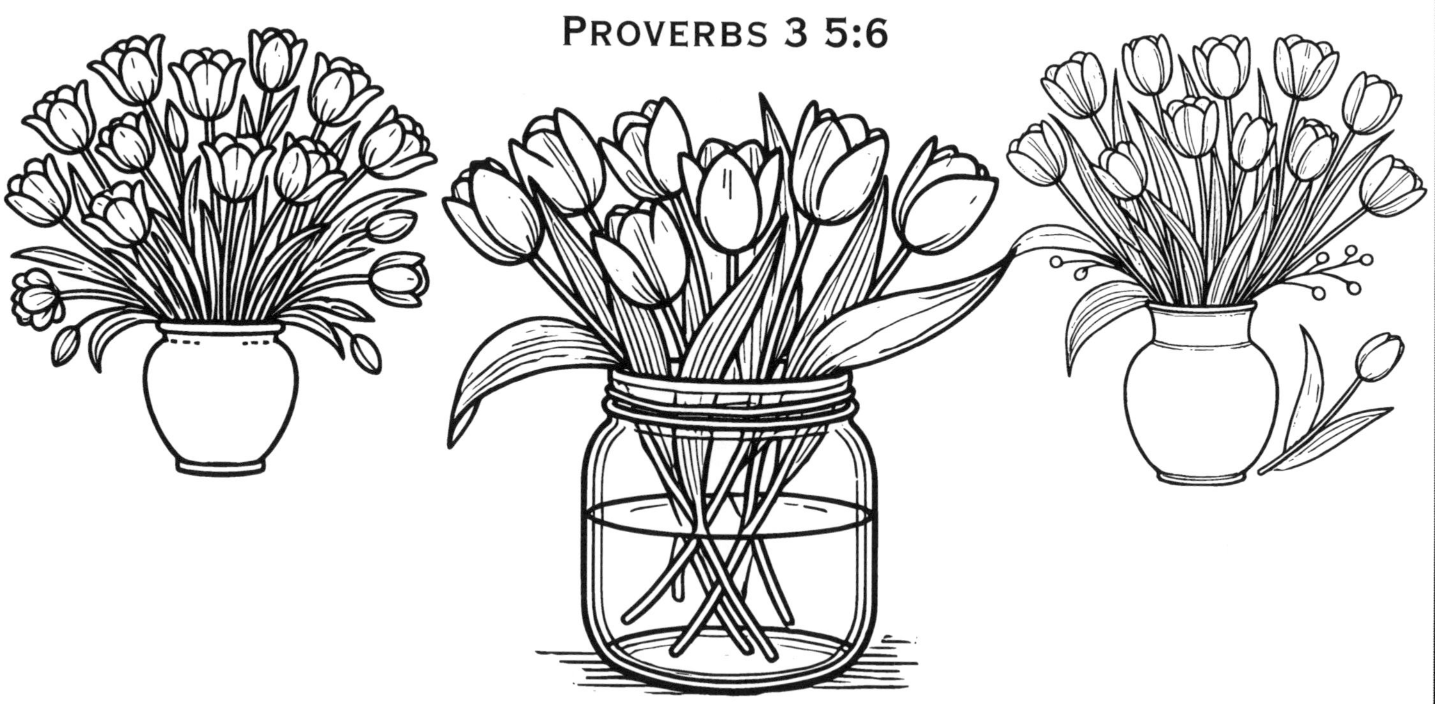

Faith is more than just believing in God; it's about trusting in His goodness and His promises, even when the road ahead seems unclear. Trusting in God requires letting go of the need to control everything and surrendering to His will. We are not meant to figure everything out on our own. Instead, we are to trust in Him completely with our hearts, minds, and lives. We often juggle so many roles and responsibilities in our day to day, and can easily become overwhelmed and begin relying on our own strength. But when we lean on our own strength, we miss the wisdom that comes from God. Trusting in His ways means letting go of the need for perfection, releasing anxiety about the unknown, and surrendering our fears to Him.

Heavenly Father, thank you for the gift of peace that comes from trusting in You. Help me to keep my mind fixed on You, especially when life feels uncertain or overwhelming. May Your peace fill my heart and mind, guiding me through every challenge I may face. I trust in Your faithfulness and ask for Your presence to surround me today.
In Jesus' name, Amen.

WORDS FROM THE SPIRIT

"Now faith is confidence in what we hope for and
assurance about what we do not see."
Hebrews 11:1

WORDS FROM THE SPIRIT

"And we know that in
all things God works
for the good of those
who love him, who have
been called according
to his purpose."
Romans 8:28

WORDS FROM THE SPIRIT

"Take delight in the
Lord , and he will
give you the desires
of your heart."
Psalm 37:4

Words from the Spirit

"Do not be anxious about anything, but
in every situation, by prayer and
petition, with thanksgiving, present
your requests to God. And the peace of
God, which transcends all
understanding, will guard your hearts
and your minds in Christ Jesus."
Philippians 4:6-7

Words from the Spirit

THE END

COLOR TEST PAGE

COLOR TEST PAGE

Made in the USA
Columbia, SC
06 May 2025